Playing Outside

For Shannon –
Another lover of
poetry. I hope you
enjoy these!
All best wishes,
Lucia
3/21/06

poems by
Lucia Galloway

Finishing Line Press
Georgetown, Kentucky

Playing Outside

To the memory of my father,
Gerald Benson Galloway,
who encouraged my love of language
and taught me how to play.

This is a limited collector's edition.

ACKNOWLEDGMENTS

The following poems previously appeared under the name Lucia (Anne) Dick in magazines:

"Towards Evening, Overcast," "Ceremony," "Dark Matter," "Our Turn," and "Terminus" appeared in *Cumberland Poetry Review*

"Our Turn" won the 1997 Bread Loaf Poetry Prize of the Bread Loaf School of English

"The Voice of the Air" appeared in *Full Circle*

"Roller Skating with Walt Whitman" appeared in *The Crimson Crane*

"Ourselves, Afraid" appeared in *The Review: Sierra Nevada College*

Editor: **Leah Maines**

Author Photo: **J. A. Penn**

Cover Art: Original art by **Thomas Allen** entitled "Uplift" courtesy Foley Gallery, New York

Printed in the USA on acid-free paper. ♻

Order online: **www.finishinglinepress.com**
also available on amazon.com

Author inquiries and mail orders:

Finishing Line Press
P. O. Box 1626
Georgetown, Kentucky 40324
U. S. A.

Table of Contents

Towards Evening, Overcast

Inverted green foliage,
Sky's flannel gray hue—
This pond is a mirror.
What more can I do

When glimpsing my face
In its specular view
Than admit myself double,
Both wanton and true.

Demoiselles

demoiselle: 1. A young lady. 2. An Old World crane, *Anthropoides Virgo*, having gray and black plumage and white plumes at the side of the head. 3. A damselfly.

You'll see us in our 21-inch skirts
(that's just below mid-thigh)
compressing the fat above the knees
with trendy tights the color of our boots.
We've learned to eschew the fishnet stockings,
not that they couldn't work, but flab is sly.

We grace the unlikeliest of urban centers
not just the art openings, the up-scale malls.
We line the streets at ticker-tape parades.
In church we tap-tap down the aisles
in strap-y sandals with stiletto heels.

Sleek leather pants and jackets soft as putty
dare them to think we're over fifty!
slung like folded wings across the back and shoulders,
revealing leopard-printed tops on torsos
shimmery as a damsel fly's, as nifty.

We are a sisterhood of Old World cranes,
our plumage, could you see it, tinged with gray.
Indeed, we flaunt a white streak at each temple
as we arrive at Bloomingdales to shop,
ready to pursue our peregrine play.

Ceremony

For Two Married at the Candlelight Wedding Chapel, Reno

A peal of laughter underneath the stair,
The floating petals where their voices dropped,
And always the style, the spin, that certain flair.

Beneath the fog, the early chefs despair
While lovers whinny as if sleep had cropped
A peal of laughter underneath the stair.

Twin candelabras' pristine wicks declare
That flames cost extra. Still they can adopt
The city's glitz: its style, that certain spin and flair.

The driver earns no salary: peevish wear
And tear on nuptial glee, which roguishly concocts
A peal of laughter underneath the stair.

For baking, body building, bicycle repair
She puts away her fashionable sequined tops.
But always the style, the spin, that certain flair.

They live the lives of lovers sipping air
Or smoothies; lounge on pillows propped.
A peal of laughter underneath the stair
And always the style, the spin, that certain flair.

Poem Without the Piano

for Jeremy

You can't always keep things
from spilling out of the piano.
Even if you're expecting
just notes—
in tunes and rills,
chords and counterpoint—
you may get minnows silvered,
darting in little schools,
or sumo wrestlers panting,
groaning with the contest.
You may get Chinese acrobats
stacked up in pyramids
or paddle balls
or yo-yos
whirligigs
Pick-up-Stix
painted turtles
crawling from the fissures
between the keys.
Things whose happening takes shape
in the spaces between sounds.

The Voice of the Air

after the picture by Magritte

The air in my study hisses, *sotto voce*,
like the gas burner on my kitchen stove,
before the flame ignites. I go down
and start to measure tea leaves
into the strainer basket. Then wait
until the kettle goes crazy with its whistle,
sounding off. Shrill voice of air escaping,
like the noise a factory whistle makes
at noon. We take our tea onto the deck, where
the sky's a raucous call and answer hurled
from throat to throat. The crows are at it.
Surrounded by groves and fields, a distant
road under a cloudless dome, we've stepped
into Magritte's pastoral. Above,
glancing and rebounding, giant globes,
like billiard balls in a three-dimensional field.
Except it's hard to say whether
they've ever been in motion, so static do they
now appear in their suspension.
One thing seems certain, though: they speak, have spoken.
Those slots bisecting each circumference let them
inhale and exhale, call and answer.
They seem a kind of chime the air is pregnant with
while we are gravid with their music.
Imperceptibly, we've grown heavy
with gestation. The deep reverberations,
the crisp garrulity of crows.

Roller Skating with Walt Whitman

Just think how much more of Manhattan
You could see, Walt!
Come. Don this pair of skates.
Strap these wheels to your feet.
Let the roughness of the pavement vibrate through your bones.
Let the push of your legs and the swing of your arms propel you.
Let your gaze be far and near,
Seeing the skyscrapers and sidewalk cracks,
Seeing the sunset reflected in many windows
And the dapper missionaries with their tracts.
Seeing the grand marquees and the Good Humor men,
And the beggars in their patient bodies,
And the noble statuary, and pigeons strutting in the squares.
Seeing stylish women with their handbags
And plain women pulling carts.
Put your skates on, Walt,
And follow me.
Or if you lead, I will follow,
Whirling with you in the ranks of multitudes,
Finding myself in the streamers of your hatband
Flying in the wind.

Those Rainy Mondays

Brash and naked,
you stand shameless
in your newness
inside the block walls
of the old foundation
behind
the furnace,
between
a rust-stained sink
and a drain hole
in the floor.
Monday mornings
Mother leaves
the kitchen's warmth and light,
descends the narrow
stairs,
bearing offerings
of underwear and aprons,
towels
bed sheets,
tablecloths.
Unlike the furnace,
that hearty old trunk
that sends its air ducts
branching across
the ceiling,
you have just one
bold flower,
a wringer.
Stiff and serviceable,
it looks more sinister
than song inducing.
We children circle
the basement
on our skates
while Mother
feeds the wringer's maw.
We hear
the suck of water,

thump
of the dowel
with which she stuffs
the wringer's lips.
Watch it gobble up
each juicy bit
she offers
then swivel
forty-five degrees
to repeat the sequence
over tubs of rinse.
There's never any question
who's in charge.
And not until
it's time
to shake out sheets
do we find usefulness
in this routine.
We hold
the edges
while our mother
clasps the wooden pins
between her teeth,
raises one corner
to the line
and then
the heavy middle
then the end.
How we love to skate
through humid
corridors
between the lines
of sheets
then burst out,
flapping wings!
These rainy Mondays
we spin
'round and 'round
on concrete
to the hum and gentle rumble
of the wash machine.

Thomas Hart Benton Paints the Hailstorm

Raptured
in that instant when
lighting forks down, and
stumps and grasses blanch
with phosphorescence—
who has not wished it?
It's heaven and hell at once:
familiarity subverted in undersea forms:
undulating leaves and octopus stumps,
the air grown sulphurous and heavy,
the great rocks porous, spongy.
It's the mayhem that we crave—
wind so strong the very world bends
and man and beast are bent on finding
shelter, even while
yearning to be taken.

Benton's mule charges toward the shed.
Wind-driven thunderheads charge
the pearly resident sky
like purple-green dragons humping their backs and hissing
fire. The gnarled tree's turned bestial
in collusion, flinging leaves like flames
from the mouths of its tossing boughs.
Heaven's on the horizon,
if only we could get there
across the field's rich corduroy furrows
straining toward the light
bowed in darkness.

Dark Matter

Space and stars in great galactic wheels
Not dense enough in mass, in gravitas,
To hold together in a *universe*.
And yet we have it. The paradox appeals
To the astronomer, who eats his fast-food meals
In the observatory, or rushing off to class
Expounds his dearly-won hypothesis
Before the random face whose pout but half conceals
Her boredom. There must be something more
(we're back to the universe now, take note)
To make the grand collage of stuff cohere.
And now, *dark matter!* Think of plugs too dense to float,
Those used-up stars that fill the empty center—
Dark donut holes that hold the rim together.

Playing Outside

The grade-school playground:
a lot done
with steel pipes,
with elbow joints & t's,
socketed joints like v's—
the framework for swings
that hung from creaking, clanking
chains. The monkey bars,
their horizontals polished
to a dull patina by
the undersides of knees,
the jungle gym, its stern
geometry.

Fat, aluminum-painted pipe
with feet cemented in the ground
made the fulcrum for the teeter-
totter's bleached gray boards
grown splinter-y in the sun.
Precarious to mount the see-saw
when, at opposite ends,
you & your playmate
leveled the board
& throwing one leg over,
eased your buttocks down.
No handles there to grasp,
only the fist-sized indentations cut
into the board's sides.

It took some kind of nerve
when forward-pitched
at 45 degrees
you looked
your playmate in the eye,
tried not to grimace
when your body bounced,
lifting your rear end off the board
as his end hit the gravel.
It took a timing fine
as any surfer's
to settle back a little sooner,

shifting your weight to lift him
to the balance point
and past, gaining
the momentum of the fall,
then absorbing it into your legs,
your knees
to soften the tooth-jarring jolt
of your end's touching.

Alone some Sunday at the playground,
the place your aimless steps had led,
restless, you'd start to climb
the angled teeter-totter board
from grounded base to airy precipice.
Then all muscles tensed
as you leveled the whole tilted yard
at the crux—
a split-second mastery
before the onus fell.

Our Turn

When we, as children, sat at Mother's table
And heard the talk that circled round the board—
Which aunt had put up pears, and who was able
To can a mess of beans and still accord
Some time to sewing for the Ladies' Aid,
Which man had suffered illness, which one tossed
Away his life just as his debts were paid:
These things we learned and scarcely knew our loss;
We passed the days and hoped that we might earn
The privilege of speaking out of turn.

We children asked the blessing for the meal
That kept us sitting up in straight-back chairs.
We must not squirm, or ask for a repeal
Of clean-plate laws. Impertinent who dares
To challenge the decorum grown-ups need.
And so we pushed our peas around our plates,
Not having, really, any case to plead,
And chewed on scraps of weather, haystacks, hates.
We passed the hours and thought that we would spurn
Such niceties of discourse in our turn.

Feet

Down in the church basement
women my mother's age
were rolling down their nylon hose,
peeling them off
and tucking each balled-up stocking
into a waiting shoe.
We witnessed from the sidelines,
Barb and I—too small to sit alone in the pew,
our gender wrong to go along with Dad.
We hadn't any other choice
than looking at them—
feet white as bread or Gruyere cheese
beneath the crusts and rinds of calluses,
bunioned feet, embossed with corns;
some rosy as trout
wriggling in the basin
before submitting to another woman's hands,
the swathe of water, the caress.

Palm Sunday morning, this rite of Mennonites
unfolded from below the stairs in even cadences
of water poured from pitchers
soles massaged in rough thin towels:
women washing one another's feet
while chords swelled their permutations—
those G major hymns overwhelming the stairwell,
marching toward their resolutions.

Each time I hear an organ being played,
I think of this, and yet another memory:
my mother's sturdy feet
marching me down the basement corridors of Presser Hall
through cavernous dissonance
toward Miss Newcomb's studio.

Miss Newcomb sat beside the grand piano
administering corrections
or awarding stars. Soon I'd be
the kid on the bench, watching from

14

the corner of my eye Miss Newcomb
lift the glasses from her ample breast
and shake her jowls a little as she adjusted the specs upon her
nose.
For now, I had a brief reprieve
to wander 'round the studio
reading for the umpteenth time
quotations she had taped to the studio door,
We boil at different temperatures. —Emerson
The afternoon light
faded from the high basement windows
and the feet of college students passed outside.
The moon shown bright on Mrs. Porter
And on her daughter
They washed their feet in soda water. —Eliot

When I went to lessons by myself,
taking the bus from school,
after an hour of scales and Bach
I left the studio at dusk,
walked the blocks to the bus stop,
waited under thickening skies, legs raw in the wind,
feet freezing on the blackened ice,
counting the makes of cars to Haydn's measures,
watching for the headlights of the bus,
afraid to fathom any basement rites—
pressing of toes or piano keys.
And the lush cadences
drawing me evenly, inevitably
toward the footfalls of my kind.

Ourselves, Afraid

It's hard not to notice the way
a funeral makes order
of the uncertainty of our lives.
How, emerging from our bedrooms
in best black dress or suit, we feel formal
and composed, as if contained
in picture frames. Like the dead,
today we make no decisions. We are encased
in custom, instructed where to sit, when to stand.
Our trumpets of individual style
are muted by decorum, and we are carried
on the long sea swell of words and music
as if we might continue to avoid
the vertiginous drop.
We know, and do not know
as bodies that in their internal resonance learn
the voices of a fugue.

Terminus

A bubble bursts at once, lets loose its scarf—
that flimsy, filmy, quivering, liquid sphere—
and gone, the ethereal lair, the gaseous turf
once sovereign, single, integral of air.
She laughed and put away the slippers, cloaks
lace jabots, jaunty hats, the headed cane
with which she tapped the tempered trunks of oaks—
she wouldn't need to use these props again—
then followed through the dawn on paths of ice
migrants or pilgrims bearing poems and glosses
(the sunlight glinted coldly off the glass
of spectacles set neatly on their noses).
And not a cricket chirred or bird ascended,
nothing at all to signal what had ended.

Soft Parts

for Laurie

"I'm making slugs from snails," you said,
a deft blow from the rock in your hand
smashing down on the whorl of another shell
to liberate its naked occupant. You were just
four or five. We thought you precocious.

Did we think also of the body cast you'd worn
in babyhood to realign your hips and thighs?
Your tummy must have itched inside your plaster shell.
I think of the chafe of your ankles against the cuffs
of chalk and gauze, the rigid tights that sheathed your legs.

Snails take shelter in the vestibules of spiral shells,
coming out to make their transient, iridescent trails.
You couldn't slither out, although you'd use
your arms and feet, turtle-like, to move across the floor.

I couldn't even diaper you, take your ankles in one hand
to slide the folded cloth under your little bum,
but had to invent a way to fit the cut-down Pampers
into the oblong hole in the crotch of your cast.
I missed the stack of 4-ply cotton diapers,
lost track of the pink-headed diaper pins.

I lost the touch of bath water gloving my hands,
washing the fold of skin inside each baby thigh;
the nesting of you, damp and warm, against me, your shape
conforming to mine as I held you to my chest.
The hooded towel I'd toss around you—lost that too.

I keep this litany of what I lost because in no way
could I own the shell you kept around you. Not
experience your tenancy or penetrate its privacy:
the dark safety of your knees, their dimples cosseted.
Your hips and thighs arranged just so,
your buttocks pressed as smooth as pillows in a drawer.

18

Shells I know by their outer surfaces:
horny, hard to the touch, alien,
but to their owners, homes—yes, fortresses.
To bunker and body armor do small creatures
entrust their soft parts—the snails and turtles,
crabs and lobsters, beetles, armadillos.

And you, now in your adulthood, your shell
nearly invisible and paper-thin between us:
your letters durable and correct, even in their
girded irony, their carapace of wit. In parchment
envelopes they come, with my address
scripted in careful lines across the front.

Ginseng on Court Street

In memory of Josephine D'Esposito, 1927-2004

1. Disproportion

Respite from being useful was
what mattered to me then amidst
the disproportion of a family Christmas
in the homes of my grown-up children—
clearing the breakfast table,
pouring their cups of tea.

I found it sauntering the Brooklyn streets
in Carroll Gardens: Court Street shops
of tailors, bakers, stationers, and sellers
of used dishes—those old Italians ready to chat
or cheat me when I poked in to nose around.

2. Josie Pours Half-and-Half

Ancient athletic pants and a worn fleece pullover,
two white braids dangling beside her ears from the plush
of a red velveteen cap—I wanted her to be
Mrs. Claus in Brooklyn. She nailed me for a stranger
as I crossed her threshold. "Josie Java," she hollered,
"Gotta pee." And she left me standing amidst the tinsel,
colored lights, the small unhopeful Santas dressed in dingy velvet.
I found a place to sit at one of the mismatched tables.

Josie presided from her counter perch
and barked my order to her cook, got up
to serve my eggs and bacon on a paper plate.
Her only grace was whitening my *cauffee.*
"Say when." And then she wheeled around,
reclaimed her right to gossip with the regulars,
relished some news of the day: a Chinese woman mugged.
"They went into her boobs for it," Josie howled.

3. Demography

Once it would have been an Irish Christmas.
For some time, though, the Caputos and Friellos, the Raccuglias
and the Leones have set the tone in Carroll Gardens.
Josie's Java held its place on Court Street in the block between
Frank Caputo's cheese shop and St. Mary Star of the Sea.

Last June, inside a letter from my daughter
a tribute clipped from the New York Times
to Josie and her place. For us, that dim establishment a novelty:
neither of us had been there more than once.

Imagine, then, Memorial Day, the grate down
before the door of Josie's shop and mass being said for her,
dead of a heart attack at 76.   Dead after pouring countless cups,
dead after calling me *Sweetheart*. After adding the price
of the daily paper to my tab and squabbling with the
customer who brought his own to read while sipping.

4. A Sense of Place

"I'll miss her, yelling over there," said Andy Cho,
businessman, from his health-food emporium
across the street from Josie's Java. Maybe Mr. Cho
stopped in at Josie's wake, placing a pot of white chrysanthemums
beside the gaudy sprays of long-stemmed gladiolas,
murmuring condolences with eyes lowered to the shoes
of Josie's four grown sons. Maybe.

It's Josie's *moxie* that I'm thinking of.
That raw December day, the lights of Christmas winking
and her harsh notes sounding, already of the past:
a moment distant enough for two strangers to meet,
reluctant hostess, nosey guest. I had stepped into her place
to forget whatever it was that kept us pouring.

Meadowlands

Meadows is its name—
cornfields abutting the highway into town,
grain elevator alongside the tracks.
Pastures skirt the outlying barns and sheds,
where cows may graze. An elder-care facility
runs its ramps down to the walks and well-cut lawns.
Each village house presides over its plot of grass.

In my dreamscape, Meadows isn't green—
not pastoral but proud, and hard with pavement.
Stone alleys, their sharp turns opening into
narrow courtyards, rough-hewn uneven steps
ascending to sun-baked terraces.
The only verdure is the weeds pushing through
crevices, hairy thistles sporting their purple flowers.

Clambering over cobbles, hugging the scant shade of walls,
I stop when suddenly given a small sun-powered car.
With this vehicle, I see a way
to gain the freeway, which, I'm told,
leads to the evergreen forest where, in a cool glade
families are feasting. But fortune here is meager . . .

Missing the turn to the access road—misconstruing
the on-ramp for an avenue—I'm routed into a maze of narrow,
rutted paths where every turn and twist takes me
farther from the torrid surfaces, deeper, to discover
a town's wet core. Here in its teeming cellar
I've no other course but to pay homage
to the savage greening of the meadowlands,
the non-negotiable energy rising from roots and stems.

Pain

1.

Dirt warm as ash recedes at a cavern's mouth
that Yorgos entered to escape the Aegean sun.
He squats in the cave's cool hall, he feels a knob,
begins to dig and gradually scrapes
the soil from her astonished torso
still hiding its lovely torque in the modest clay.
He bears the object in his sun-burnt arms—
his earthy gift—into the light. His sun and moon,
his Aphrodite. But she'll be taken from him
to illuminate the grand stair at the Louvre—
Venus de Milo, perfect, armless,
abiding the viewer's gaze.

2.

My own arm screaming from my cousin's
twisting it up behind my back.
(Are all boys such callow playmates?)
This same kid made me ride the handlebars
while he rode zig-zag on the bike, fast
around the oval track, and I needed
the strength of both my arms
to keep from flying off.

3.

The muscles in her legs and belly tense;
the gathers of her tunic press against
her thighs. Iris, the flying messenger, cropped
from the west pediment of the Parthenon,
alights without the help of either wings or arms
on the fake Acropolis erected
at the British Museum. Last night
I dreamt my infant daughter had been thrown
into a barrel, and I, armless,
could not rescue her.

4.

A son supported in his mother's arms,
dead across her lap—the Pieta.

5.

The mother hovers near him, registering
his pain: her son, the climber, had cut off his arm
to cripple death. One hand pinned
beneath a boulder, he'd snapped the arm bones
with the other, sawed through radius and ulna,
like a cook disjointing chicken with a dull knife.

6.

I want to rub my broken arm with dirt
from the pit in the holy room where slings
and crutches line the walls. The Santuario
de Nuestro Senor. Tiny amulets of tin some call
milagros are for sale on streets converging
on the place of healing—miniature legs and feet,
those little arms.

7.

Four arms of the dancing Siva: two
to hold the drum and flame, a third
to gesture benediction. A fourth
arm promises relief from suffering.

About the Author

A native of the Illinois prairie, Lucia Galloway was educated in Illinois, Ohio, Kansas, and California. She earned the M.A. in English from the University of California, Berkeley (1964), and taught English and American literature at the high-school and college levels for almost twenty years. She began writing poetry seriously after participating as a Fellow in a National Institute for the Humanities Seminar on Emily Dickinson and Walt Whitman (1993). In the summer of 1997 she studied poetry with Paul Muldoon at the Bread Loaf School of English, where she won the Robert Haiduke Poetry Prize. She holds the MFA in Creative Writing from Antioch University, Los Angeles (2002). Her poems have appeared in a number of print and on-line journals, among them *Columbia Poetry Review, Cumberland Poetry Review, The Crimson Crane, Flyway, Full Circle, The Lyric, Poetry Midwest, The Sierra Nevada Review,* and *Spillway.* Presently, she teaches in the Distance Writing Program of the Johns Hopkins University Center of Talented Youth. She lives with her husband in the university town of Claremont, California. They are the parents of three grown daughters.